J.M Black

Stegosaurus

Stegosaurus

Heather Amery

Illustrated by Tony Gibbons

DINOSAUR COLLECTION

PARRAGON

Contents

Introducing Stegosaurus

Stegosaurus (STEG-OH-SAW-RUS) was a large and strange-looking dinosaur whose bones have been found in North America. It may have seemed fierce but was really very peaceful. However, it could put up a good fight if attacked by one of the giant, meat-eating dinosaurs who thought it would make a good meal.

The double row of plates along its back, ending in a spiked tail, puzzled scientists for a long time. What were they for? Were they perhaps used to protect **Stegosaurus** from the teeth and claws of other dinosaurs? Or did **Stegosaurus** use the plates to cool down or warm up its body?

Could it move them, and even lay them down flat? Or were they just for decoration?

And, scientists have asked, since **Stegosaurus** had such a small brain, was it the most stupid dinosaur of all?

You will find the answers to many questions about **Stegosaurus** on the pages that follow.

5

Spot one!

Stegosaurus is quite easy to recognize because of the rows of plates that stick up all the way along its body.

It was a big dinosaur, about as long as two large cars. You would probably only have come up to about its knees.

Its back legs were about twice as long as its front legs, and it plodded slowly along, with its head fairly close to the ground.

The other very noticeable thing about **Stegosaurus** was its tail. It was a powerful, thick tail – with long spikes – which tapered towards the end. **Stegosaurus** swished it from side to side as it moved.

Each spike of **Stegosaurus'** tail was about a metre in length – that is nearly as tall as you are. They were made of bone and were very sharp, making useful weapons for self-defence when an enemy approached. **Stegosaurus** often had to protect itself against fierce predators who fancied a meal of its flesh.

Stegosaurus only had a small, narrow head that was tiny compared with its body. Its mouth had a beak. Since it was a herbivore, eating only vegetation, it used this to tear off all the soft plants, leaves and ferns that it ate. **Stegosaurus** chewed these up with the rows of small, weak teeth that were at the back of its jaw. It probably stored its food for several days in a large stomach.

7

Magnificent skeleton

From its remains, we know **Stegosaurus** had very strong bones to hold up the weight of its heavy body. But the most surprising thing about its structure are the two rows of large, flat plates which stood upright on its neck, all the way along its back and then right down its tail.

These plates were smaller near its head and towards the tail. The largest plates were in the middle of its back.

The plates were made of bone but not fixed to the main skeleton. At the end of the tail were the four sharp spikes that **Stegosaurus** used for self-defence.

8

When **Stegosaurus** was first discovered, scientists were puzzled by something about its skeleton.

Later, however, other scientists decided that the hole held lumps of a chemical called glycogen. Some animals and birds alive today also have glands that release this chemical. It supplies their muscles with extra energy when they need to fight or run away from enemies or danger.

Stegosaurus also needed to call on extra supplies of energy to defend itself against predators.

What was the space in its backbone, near its hips? Some thought that **Stegosaurus** might have had another brain there to control its huge body. (Its head, as you can see, was tiny in comparison with the rest of its body, and the brain in its head was the smallest of all the dinosaurs that have been discovered so far.)

Stegosaurus had stumpy feet, like an elephant. It plodded along on all fours but could also stand on its back legs to feed from trees. Its legs were designed to support its weight, not for speedy running. So, if a hungry carnivore approached, **Stegosaurus** would not have had much success in escaping, but would have had to fight for its life.

9

When Stegosaurus

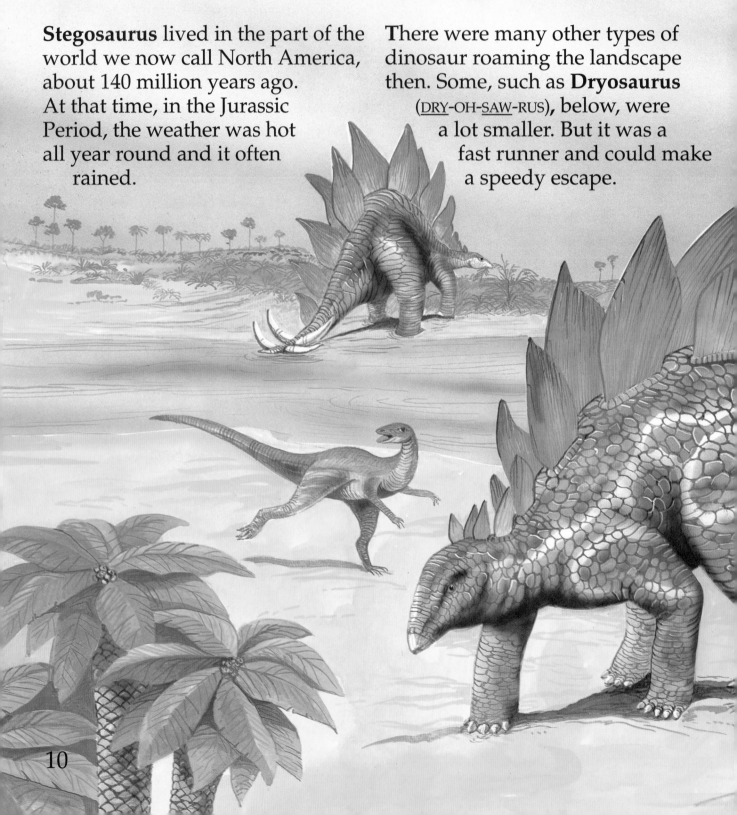

Stegosaurus lived in the part of the world we now call North America, about 140 million years ago. At that time, in the Jurassic Period, the weather was hot all year round and it often rained.

There were many other types of dinosaur roaming the landscape then. Some, such as **Dryosaurus** (DRY-OH-SAW-RUS)**,** below, were a lot smaller. But it was a fast runner and could make a speedy escape.

walked the Earth

The **Kentrosaurus** (<u>KEN</u>-TRO-<u>SAW</u>-RUS), at the bottom right hand corner of this page, was a smaller cousin of **Stegosaurus**. The dinosaur in the water is a giant, long-necked **Brachiosaurus** (<u>BRAK</u>-EE-OH-<u>SAW</u>-RUS).

Meat-eating dinosaurs hid in the thickets, waiting to take slower dinosaurs by surprise.

Bone wars

The bones of **Stegosaurus** were first dug up by workers helping a famous American scientist called Othniel C. Marsh. That was about 120 years ago. He had sent teams of men to search for dinosaurs in the wild, rugged country in Colorado and Wyoming, in the United States. They spent years hacking skeletons out of solid rock. It was hard, dangerous work.

At the same time, another famous American scientist – Edward D. Cope – sent fossil hunters to the same parts of the country.

The two men were rivals, both racing to be the first to find and name new dinosaurs.

The two teams often worked only a few kilometres apart. Sometimes they even fought over the dinosaur remains that they dug up. The rivalry between Marsh and Cope soon became known as the 'Bone Wars'.

Both scientists were very successful. Before they started their great search, only nine types of dinosaur were known to have lived in North America. But between them, these men found 136 different ones. These included the long-necked **Diplodocus** (DIP-LOD-OH-KUS) and fierce **Allosaurus** (AL-OH-SAW-RUS).

Marsh once even found that Cope had put the head on the wrong end of a dinosaur skeleton when reconstructing it! Cope was very embarrassed by his silly mistake.

13

Plated dinosaur

Stegosaurus' bony plates are a puzzle. When scientists discovered the first skeletons, they did not know if the plates lay flat on **Stegosaurus'** back or stood upright in rows. If they had stuck out sideways, they might have defended **Stegosaurus** against attack.

In fact, **Stegosaurus** got its name – meaning 'roof lizard' – because some scientists thought the plates lay flat like the tiles on a roof. But, today, most scientists believe that they stood up in pairs.

The plates formed a double row, right along **Stegosaurus'** back, but were not directly opposite each other.

What, then, were the plates for? Some scientists suggest that **Stegosaurus** used the plates to control its temperature so that it was never uncomfortably hot nor too cold.

They say that, in the cool mornings, **Stegosaurus** may have held its plates to the sun, to collect warmth. The plates were therefore perhaps like solar panels. But in the heat of the day, it might then have turned them sideways, using the breeze to cool it down.

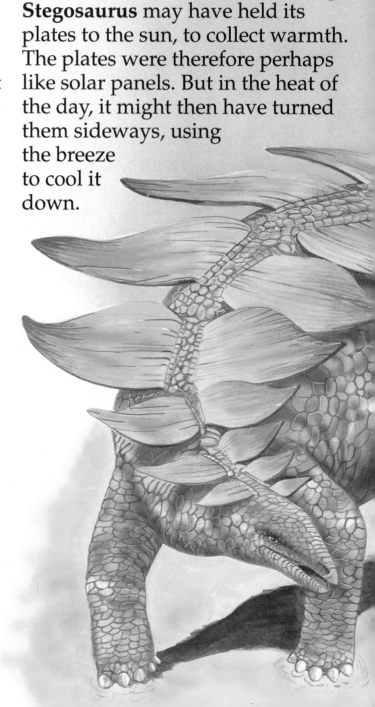

14

Blood vessels ran through these plates. They worked rather like the pipes in a central-heating system. No one is sure, however, why some types of dinosaurs needed these radiators but others did not.

There may also have been another use for the plates. Some scientists think that the plates of a male **Stegosaurus** were a very bright colour.

The plates of a female may have been smaller and less colourful.

It may have used them to attract females at the beginning of the mating season.

The magnificent plates were smallest at the neck and tail ends. They ended on the tail. Behind them, there were two pairs of bony spikes, used for self-defence against predators.

15

Life in the herd

Stegosaurus probably lived in family herds, with the older members looking after the young ones and guarding them from meat-eaters.

The herds roamed about together, looking for fresh plants and

leaves to eat once they had cleared one feeding ground of its vegetation.

They had to be on constant look-out for hungry carnivores who might attack for food at any time.

But what if a **Stegosaurus** was attacked by a meat-eater?

Then, the whole of the herd would come to the rescue, rushing to help it in its hour of need. They would lash the predator with their tails and wound it with

After two males challenged each other, they may have charged, lashing their tails and swaying their necks from side to side, crashing shoulder to shoulder and slipping about on muddy ground.

The winner then displayed its more brightly

the sharp spikes. It may have taken three of them to ward off an enemy successfully.

At the start of the mating season each year, the males may have fought each other for the females.

coloured plates to the females in order to attract them, while the loser plodded away.

Putting up a fight

Stegosaurus plodded quietly along, grazing on ferns. Suddenly, there was a terrifying roar. An **Allosaurus** crashed out of the trees and went straight for **Stegosaurus**, snapping its huge jaws. It was after a meal. And **Stegosaurus** looked appetizing.

Allosaurus was a fearsome predator, and far bigger than **Stegosaurus.** It had a massive head and vast jaws with many sharp teeth.

Stegosaurus had wandered off from the rest of the herd, and so there were no others to protect it against this predator.

Who would strike first? **Allosaurus** gave another threatening roar and leapt at **Stegosaurus.**

Stegosaurus would not give up without a fight, however. It lashed its tail at Allosaurus' stomach, the spikes gashing the predator's scaly skin.

Allosaurus clawed back viciously. Stegosaurus lashed its spiked tail again, giving Allosaurus' leg a stunning blow. Both creatures roared angrily.

Allosaurus staggered but managed to close its jaws on Stegosaurus' back. Sadly, Stegosaurus was no match for this ferocious carnivore.

19

Stegosaurus data

Stegosaurus was a very large, four-footed, plant-eating dinosaur. It had a long body, tiny head, thick tail and two rows of plates along its neck and back. It plodded along slowly on clumsy feet, its heavy, spiked tail held out behind it.

Tiny brain

Stegosaurus had a brain that was the smallest, compared with the size of its body, of any animal that has ever lived. It was only about as big as a walnut. With such a tiny brain, **Stegosaurus** could not have been very bright – but was probably clever enough for its needs.

Small head

Stegosaurus had a very small head for the size of its body. It was only about as big as a large dog's. It also had a toothless beak made of horn, which it used for chopping off the leaves on which it fed. Its nostrils were on the top of its head.

Cheek teeth

At the sides of **Stegosaurus'** jaws were small, weak cheek teeth. It probably did not chew at its meals. Instead, it swallowed stones, which it then used for grinding up food in its stomach.

Lashing tail

Stegosaurus' tail was thick and strong. Near the tip were four bony spikes. These were like built-in weapons. Any predator would have felt their sharp lash. **Stegosaurus** could also prop itself up on its tail when it stood on its back legs to feed from tall trees.

Clumsy feet

Stegosaurus had five toes on each of its front feet, and four toes on each of its back feet. The claws on its toes were like small hoofs. These hoofs were no good for fighting but may have been useful for getting a grip on very wet or muddy ground, as **Stegosaurus** lumbered along through the Jurassic landscape.

Bony plates

The largest plate on **Stegosaurus'** back was about three times the size of this page. The plates were made of bone, with lots of blood vessels around them. The plates were covered with horn or tough, scaly skin. Many scientists agree that they were probably used to control **Stegosaurus'** body temperature.

21

The Stegosaurid family

Stegosaurus was one of a family, or group, of dinosaurs called **Stegosaurids.** This name means 'roof lizards'. All members of this family had large, bony plates or spikes right the way along their backs.

Stegosaurus (1) was the largest member of this family and had the biggest plates. It lived in what we now call North America, about 140 million years ago.

Kentrosaurus (2) was a similar **Stegosaurid** – but only about half as long as **Stegosaurus**. Its name means 'pointed lizard' and it had plates on its neck, too. There were spikes on its back and tail, and on its hips. These were used to frighten off larger predators. It also lived about 140 million years ago, and skeletons have been found in Tanzania, East Africa.

3

4

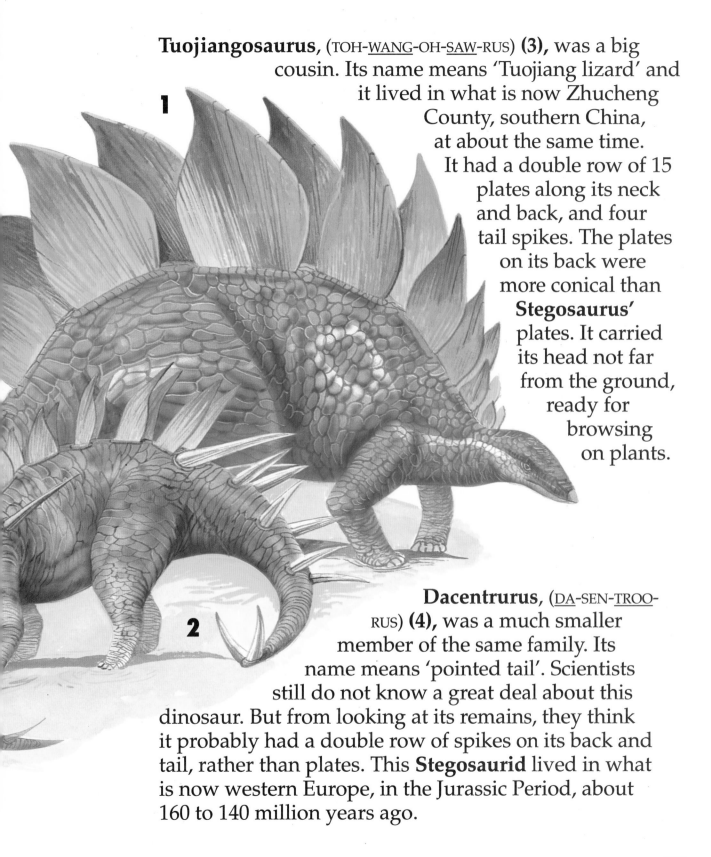

Tuojiangosaurus, (TOH-<u>WANG</u>-OH-<u>SAW</u>-RUS) **(3),** was a big cousin. Its name means 'Tuojiang lizard' and it lived in what is now Zhucheng County, southern China, at about the same time. It had a double row of 15 plates along its neck and back, and four tail spikes. The plates on its back were more conical than **Stegosaurus'** plates. It carried its head not far from the ground, ready for browsing on plants.

1

2

Dacentrurus, (<u>DA</u>-SEN-<u>TROO</u>-RUS) **(4),** was a much smaller member of the same family. Its name means 'pointed tail'. Scientists still do not know a great deal about this dinosaur. But from looking at its remains, they think it probably had a double row of spikes on its back and tail, rather than plates. This **Stegosaurid** lived in what is now western Europe, in the Jurassic Period, about 160 to 140 million years ago.

First published 1993
by Parragon Book Service, Bristol

Text and illustrations copyright
© 1993 Quartz Editorial Services
112 Station Road, Edgware HA8 7AQ

ISBN 1–85813–338–6

Printed and bound in Great Britain by BPCC Paulton Books